Presented to:

_____

From:

_____

Date:

_____

Jesus Calling®
The Story of Christmas

Sarah Young

Illustrated by Katya Longhi

Tommy NELSON®

An Imprint of Thomas Nelson

Special thanks to Mackenzie Howard for
her extensive work in shaping this manuscript.

© 2018 Sarah Young

Published in Nashville, Tennessee, by Tommy Nelson. Tommy Nelson is an imprint of Thomas Nelson. Thomas Nelson is a registered trademark of HarperCollins Christian Publishing, Inc.

Tommy Nelson titles may be purchased in bulk for educational, business, fund-raising, or sales promotional use. For information, please e-mail SpecialMarkets@ThomasNelson.com.

Unless otherwise noted, Scripture quotations are taken from the Holy Bible, New International Version®, NIV®. Copyright © 1973, 1978, 1984 by Biblica, Inc.® Used by permission of Zondervan. All rights reserved worldwide. www.Zondervan.com. The "NIV" and "New International Version" are trademarks registered in the United States Patent and Trademark Office by Biblica, Inc.® Scripture quotations marked ICB are from the International Children's Bible®. Copyright © 1986, 1988, 1999 by Thomas Nelson. Used by permission. All rights reserved. Scripture quotations marked NASB are from the New American Standard Bible®. Copyright © 1960, 1962, 1963, 1968, 1971, 1972, 1973, 1975, 1977, 1995 by The Lockman Foundation. Used by permission. (www.Lockman.org) Scripture quotations marked NKJV are from the New King James Version®. © 1982 by Thomas Nelson. Used by permission. All rights reserved. Scripture quotations marked NLT are from the Holy Bible, New Living Translation. © 1996, 2004, 2007, 2013, 2015 by Tyndale House Foundation. Used by permission of Tyndale House Publishers, Inc., Carol Stream, Illinois 60188. All rights reserved.

ISBN 978-1-4002-1029-9

Library of Congress Cataloging-in-Publication Data is on file.

Printed in China
18 19 20 21 22 DSC 10 9 8 7 6 5 4 3 2 1

Mfr: DSC / Shenzhen, China / September 2018 / PO#9503665

I dedicate this book to our grandchildren:
Elie, John, Caleb, Esther Grace, Joel, and Lawrence.
May you—and all who read this book—know
Jesus as your Savior and Friend.

Dear Parents and Grandparents,

When our children were young, our family was living in Japan, where Christmas wasn't even a holiday. People went to work and to school as usual. This actually made it easier for us to keep the emphasis in our home on Jesus' birth. On Christmas Eve, we would make a birthday cake for Jesus. Then on Christmas morning, before we opened presents, my husband would read the Christmas story to our children. Later, we'd sing "Happy Birthday" to Jesus and eat the cake we'd made to celebrate His birth.

Now we have six precious grandchildren, and we care deeply about their spiritual well-being. Christmas in the US is a whirlwind of parties and activities. The attention on giving and getting presents often takes the focus off Jesus.

This Christmas storybook is designed to help you put the emphasis on Jesus, not only as a baby in a manger, but as our Lord from the beginning of time to the end of time. It will show children that God always had a plan for Christmas, and that plan was Jesus.

I pray that this book will provide a delightful way for you to teach the children in your life about the real meaning of Christmas—the birth of Jesus, our Savior who loves us more than we can imagine!

I wish you and your family a wonderful, meaningful Christmas!

Sarah Young

Christ was there before anything was made.
And all things continue because of him.

—Colossians 1:17 ICB

The Christmas story began long, long ago. Before the angel Gabriel told Mary she would have God's Son. Before the shepherds saw the angels and before the wise men saw the star.

Even before the sun and moon shone for the first time, before the first cows ever *moooed* and the first monkeys ever climbed! Before Adam and Eve took their first walk in the garden of Eden, God had a plan for Christmas.

From the beginning of time, God's plan was Jesus!

Jesus Calling

I am the Beginning and the End. I am Jesus, God the Son. I made the heavens and the earth. Even then—long before you were born—I thought of you and I loved you.

God proclaimed this good news to Abraham long ago when he said, "All nations will be blessed through you."

—Galatians 3:8 NLT

Count the stars," God told Abraham. "That's how many children will come from you and your family!"

When Abraham was one hundred and his wife, Sarah, was ninety, God gave them a baby boy named Isaac. This promised baby was a gift to the whole world, because . . .

Abraham had Isaac.

Isaac had Jacob.

Jacob had Joseph.

Joseph had Judah . . .

And on and on the family grew, down to King David, through many more generations, and all the way to Jesus.

Jesus Calling

I am the Light of the world! Everyone who trusts Me as Savior is adopted into My royal family forever.

For a child will be born to us, a son will be given to us; and the government will rest on His shoulders; and His name will be called Wonderful Counselor, Mighty God, Eternal Father, Prince of Peace.

—Isaiah 9:6 NASB

For hundreds of years, God's prophets talked about the Savior who would come into the world to save everyone who believes in Him.

Isaiah said Jesus would be born of a pure young woman.

Micah said the Savior would be born in Bethlehem.

Hosea said that God would someday call His Son out of Egypt.

Everything happened just like they said it would.

Jesus Calling

I came into the world to break through the darkness of sin and open the gates of heaven. Nothing can change this amazing plan to save everyone who trusts in Me.

"The virgin will be pregnant. She will have a son, and they will name him Immanuel." This name means "God is with us."
—Matthew 1:23 *ICB*

God's ways and timing are always perfect. God picked just the right time for Jesus to come to earth. And He picked just the right parents for Him.

A young girl named Mary was alone one day when an angel appeared right in front of her. She couldn't believe her eyes!

"Don't be afraid, Mary," said the gentle voice of God's angel Gabriel. "God is pleased with you. Soon you will have a baby boy. His name will be Jesus. Nothing is impossible for God."

Mary trusted her Lord. "I will do whatever God wants," she told Gabriel.

Jesus Calling

Remember that I am *Immanuel*—*God with you*—and rejoice! Be happy because I have come into the world and into your life.

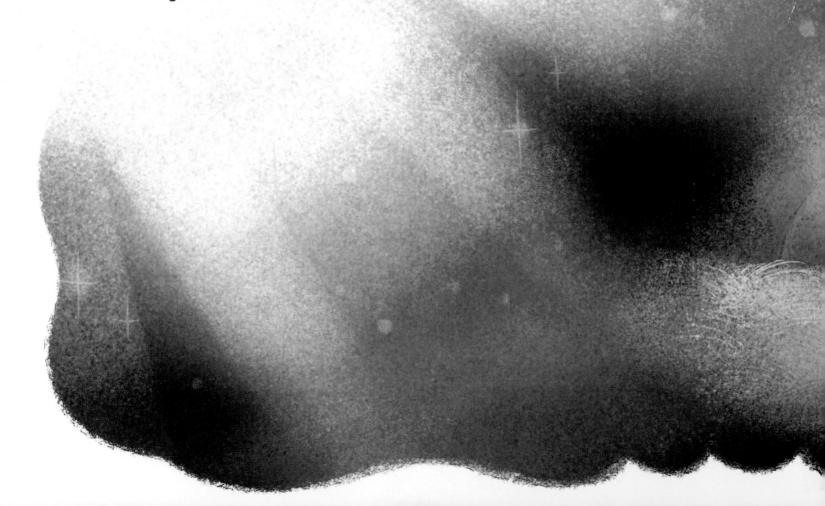

Joseph, descendant of David, don't be afraid to take Mary as your wife. The baby in her is from the Holy Spirit.
—*Matthew 1:20* ICB

Mary's fiancé, Joseph, found out she was going to have a baby before they were married. Joseph was worried.

An angel of the Lord appeared to him in a dream:

"Joseph, son of David," the angel said. "Don't be afraid to take Mary as your wife. The baby is from the Holy Spirit. Name Him Jesus because He will save His people from their sins."

When Joseph woke up, he obeyed God and did just what the angel commanded.

Jesus Calling

If you could look through My eyes—seeing
how everything fits together—you would see
how wonderfully I am caring for you. This is
why you must live by faith, not by sight—
trusting that I am with you and I love you.

"Behold, I send My messenger,
and he will prepare the way before Me."
—Malachi 3:1 NKJV

Mary's cousin Elizabeth was very old when an angel told her husband, Zechariah, that they would have a son and that they were to name him John.

John would tell people why they needed a Savior and that the One to save them was Jesus.

When Elizabeth had her baby, everyone celebrated with her and Zechariah. Then Zechariah said:

You, my little son, will be called the prophet of the Most High, because you will prepare the way for the Lord. You will tell his people how to find salvation through forgiveness of their sins.

Jesus Calling
God sent John to be a messenger who told people to repent and get ready for Me. My Father in heaven sent Me to save you from your sins. This is *very* good news!

And she gave birth to her firstborn son; and she wrapped Him in cloths, and laid Him in a manger, because there was no room for them in the inn.

—Luke 2:7 NASB

Just before Mary was about to have her baby, Joseph had to travel to his hometown, Bethlehem, to pay taxes. Bethlehem was so full of people there were no rooms left for them.

A kind innkeeper said they could stay where he kept his animals. That night, Mary had her baby. God's Son was born in a stable.

In the stillness of the night He came—God's Gift of Christmas—the One who would save the world. His mother wrapped Him in cloths and lovingly placed Him in a manger.

Jesus Calling

The message of Christmas is My birth. I gave up all the amazing riches of heaven to become a helpless baby. My birth, life, death, and resurrection allowed everyone who believes in Me to become a *child of God*.

"This will be a sign to you: You will find a baby wrapped in cloths and lying in a manger."
—Luke 2:12

In nearby fields, shepherds were watching over their flocks. Suddenly, an angel of the Lord appeared to them, and the glory of the Lord was shining around them.

"Do not be afraid," the angel said. "I bring good news that will be great joy for all people. Today, in Bethlehem—the city of David—the Savior has been born. He is the Messiah, Christ the Lord."

Suddenly, a great crowd of angels lit up the sky, praising God and saying, "Glory to God in the highest heaven, and on earth peace and good will toward men."

The shepherds ran quickly to find the baby Jesus. Then they told everyone about what they had seen and heard.

Jesus Calling

The angel's words to the shepherds were full of good news and great Joy! I came into the world to be your Savior—so you can live with Me forever.

We saw his star in the east and
have come to worship him.
—Matthew 2:2

Wise men from the East followed a bright, shining star. They visited King Herod and asked, "Where is the young child, the king of the Jews? We saw His star, and we have come to worship Him."

King Herod was not happy. "When you find Him, tell me so I can worship Him too," he lied.

The star led the wise men straight to Jesus, and they were filled with great joy!

"We have come to worship your Son," they told Mary. They presented their treasure chests of gifts—gold, frankincense, and myrrh—and bowed down to worship Him.

Jesus Calling

Christmas is the time to be joyful because it's when I came to this earth and lived in your world. I am the greatest Gift—better than all the gifts you will ever receive!

"Out of Egypt I called My son."
—Hosea 11:1 NKJV

God warned the wise men in a dream not to return to Herod, so they found a different route and set out on their journey home.

The angel of the Lord also appeared to Joseph in a dream and said, "You must escape to Egypt! Take the baby and His mother, and go quickly. King Herod has devised a plan to try to kill Jesus. You must stay until I tell you to return."

Joseph obeyed God immediately. That night, he took his little family and fled to Egypt for safety.

Jesus Calling

Be willing to follow Me wherever I lead you. Even when My way seems scary, the safest place to be is close to Me.

Believe in the Lord Jesus
and you will be saved.

—*Acts 16:31* NLT

After a while, the angel of the Lord appeared to Joseph again and said, "Get up! You can safely go back to Israel." Joseph moved his family to a town called Nazareth in Galilee.

Jesus grew up strong and wise. He taught people about God and His kingdom. Jesus loved people more than anyone who has ever lived on the earth. He died so that all the bad things we do can be forgiven and we can live forever with Him in heaven.

Jesus Calling

During this season of giving and receiving presents, remember that the very best present of all is Life that will last forever and ever. Thank Me for this wonderful gift by rejoicing and celebrating.

How great is the love the Father
has lavished on us, that we should
be called children of God!

—1 John 3:1

This Christmas, remember that God loves you so much that He sent His Son, Jesus, to the world so He could spend forever with you.

Nothing is impossible for God.

His miracles are everywhere.

God always keeps His promises.

He loves you more than you know.

God's glorious Gift of Christmas is for you.

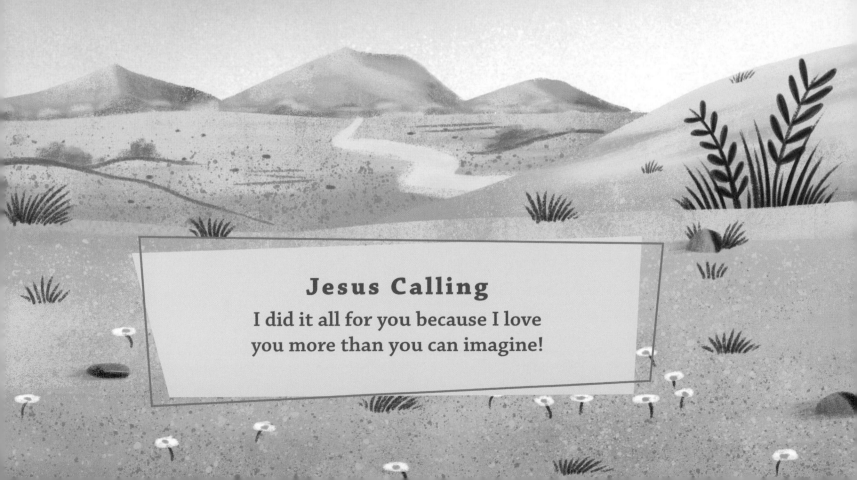

Jesus Calling

I did it all for you because I love
you more than you can imagine!

"For I am the LORD, your God, who takes hold of your right hand and says to you, Do not fear; I will help you."
—Isaiah 41:13

I AM THE LORD, YOUR GOD, but I also want to be your best Friend. As your Friend, I'm always here to help you. Together we can face whatever each day brings: good times, hard times, sad times, happy times, quiet days, and adventures.

I can be your *best* Friend because I'm perfect: I always do what is best for you. Even when you don't understand what I'm doing in your life, it's important to trust Me. Whenever you're feeling hurt or confused, try saying: "I don't understand, Jesus, but I trust You." Remember that *I'm always with you, holding you by your right hand.* I've promised to *guide you* as long as you live—and *afterward I'll take you to heaven* to live with Me forever.

It's all because I love you! My Love for you is so great that I left heaven to come into your world on that first Christmas. It's so great that I died on the cross to save you from your sins. There is no other Friend like Me!

"There is no greater love than to lay down one's life for one's friends."
—*John 15:13* NLT